What do FEELINGS look like?

Your feelings are a **BEAUTIFUL** work of art.

Happy shapes,
adventurous lines,
and energetic colors make
up your **MASTERPIECE.**

We are all different.

Every shape, color, and line has something special that makes it **UNIQUE.**

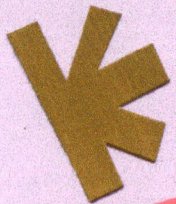

What makes **YOU** unique?

You are unique when you are
EXACTLY YOU.

It sure is AWESOME
to be YOU!

But sometimes, it can be a little hard.

Do you ever get nervous to be EXACTLY YOU?

Or worried what someone might think?

Or afraid of how you feel?

Or scared of what might happen?

Those feelings are
NORMAL.

Sometimes, those feelings are called **ANXIETY.**

It can feel like you're made up of **KNOTS** and **SCRIBBLES.**

But guess what?

Those feelings can be GOOD.

Those feelings can help you practice being

STRONG

and

BRAVE.

With practice,

your feelings can do lots of AMAZING THINGS!

Have you ever felt a little sad and gray?

Sometimes those feelings are called
DEPRESSION.

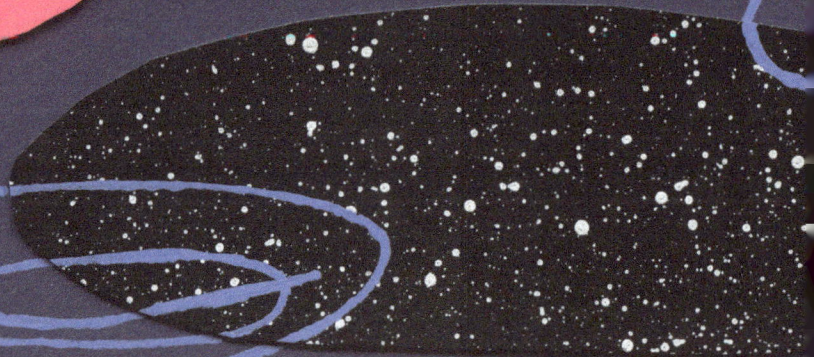

It can feel like you
live under a stormcloud.

Or that you're asleep
even when you're awake.

IT'S OKAY
to have those feelings too.

Because those feelings can help

you notice when you're

HAPPY!

Happiness
can feel warm
like the sun!

And when you feel warm like the SUN...

You can make others feel warm too.

How can you SHARE your happiness?

You can
BE KIND.

You can make it rain
KINDNESS!

What feeling helps you
spread your kindness?

CONFIDENCE!

When you believe in yourself, you feel **TALL** and **PROUD** like a mountain.

You KNOW what you are capable of.

Confident flowers don't compare themselves to other flowers.

THEY JUST
BLOOM!

Your shapes, colors, and lines dance inside you creating a BEAUTIFUL MASTERPIECE!

You are an AMAZING work of art,

and your feelings make you...

EXACTLY YOU!

ART PROJECTS

Use this book and list of art project ideas to help inspire your own creative exploration of your feelings!

Let's create!

CIRCLE OF CONTROL

- **Start:** Use a variety of art materials like crayons, oil pastels, and paints to scribble expressive lines and splatters all over your paper, filling it from edge to edge.

- **Check-in:** Do your lines express your feelings? Can you make a calm line? An anxious line? A cheerful line? Do your lines change depending on your mood?

- **Finish:** Cut out a neat circle from the middle of your scribble art. THIS is your circle of control. Your circle is filled with knots, marks, scribbles, and splashes of color, representing your feelings. Practice listing the things you can control within your circle and identifying the things you cannot control outside your circle. Display your circle proudly as a reminder to focus on what you can control and let go of the rest.

RAYS OF HAPPINESS

- **Start:** Create a happy sun using art materials such as paper collage, paint, or clay. Remember to add bold sun rays shining from your sun.

- **Check-in:** What makes you happy? What does it feel like when you're happy? Why is it important to exercise your positivity muscles?

- **Finish:** In the rays of your sun, write what makes you happy. List things that you are thankful for, people that make you feel good, and anything else that gives you that sun-shiny feeling. Display your sun in a bright spot as a reminder to flex your positivity muscles.

UNIQUE FEELINGS

- **Start:** Cut out a variety of organic and geometric shapes using colorful paper. Explore cutting edges that imitate the flow of nature and experiment with edges that are straight and sturdy. Collect your shapes into one neat stack.

- **Check-in:** Did you create paper shapes of different sizes and designs? Look through your stack, what shape best represents you today, in this moment? Why do you connect with this shape today? Check back tomorrow, do you connect with a different shape?

- **Finish:** Glue your unique shapes onto a fresh paper with each shape in its own space, not overlapping or touching any other shapes. Use your favorite art tools to draw expressive lines, scribbles, and wiggles in between your shapes. Display your feelings collage as a reminder that each of your unique feelings is beautiful.

GUIDING QUESTIONS

Use these helpful questions and the ones in this book to talk with a close family member, teacher, or friend to identify your feelings and reflect on them.

Let's talk!

- How do you FEEL right now?
- What feelings do YOU have most often? Are they positive or negative?
- What makes you feel CONFIDENT?
- When do you feel HAPPY?
- Do you ever feel ANXIOUS? What does anxiety feel like to YOU?
- How can you practice being KIND?
- Why is it important to TALK about your feelings?

Meet Sarah Krajewski!

artroomglitterfairy.com

As an elementary art educator in Wisconsin, Sarah loves creating art and being silly with her young artists. On days when using glitter in art class, Sarah sports a tiara, glitter wings, and a wand, acting as the magical art room glitter fairy! The rule is: only the glitter fairy gets to touch the glitter. It's the best kept secret for classroom glitter management.

Sarah loves creating art with bright, happy colors and abstract shapes. She uses a combination of interior house paint, acrylic inks, and metallic enamel to share positivity with the world through her art.

Sarah is an advocate for openly talking about mental health. She aims to help everyone accept, normalize, and love all types of feelings. She works this accepting mindset into her classroom by reciting a self-affirming mantra with her artists each day.

My mantra. I am positive. I am creative. I am mindful. I am amazing. I am an artist.

Published by Orange Hat Publishing 2020
ISBN 978-1-64538-191-4

For information on bulk orders or an author visit, please contact:

Orange Hat Publishing
shannon@orangehatpublishing.com
www.orangehatpublishing.com
Waukesha, WI